SIBLINGS

SCIENTISTS

FEMINISTS

JOURNALISTS

DIRECTORS

ADVENTURERS

NURSES

ENVIRONMENTALISTS

DOCTORS

CAMPAIGNERS

ARTISTS

FOR FREDDIE—because boys are brilliant too!

"Everyone has inside of him a piece of good news.
The good news is that you don't know how great you can be!"
ANNE FRANK

• First U.S. edition 2019 • First published by Walker Books Ltd. (United Kingdom) 2017 • Library of Congress Catalog Card Number pending. ISBN 978-1-5362-0111-6 • This book was typeset in Caslon Book. The illustrations were done in watercolor and ink.
Candlewick Press, 99 Dover Street, Somerville, Massachusetts 02144. visit us at www.candlewick.com.
Printed in Heshan, Guangdong, China. 19 20 21 22 23 24 LEO 10 9 8 7 6 5 4 3 2 1

# HOORAY FOR WOMEN!

WRITTEN AND ILLUSTRATED BY

## MARCIA WILLIAMS

Men do amazing, fantastic things too!

Of course they do. But there are lots of books about them already!

CANDLEWICK PRESS

# CLEOPATRA VII

## Queen of Egypt
C. 69–30 BCE

Cleo had charm.

I rule Egypt, but I speak only Greek.

Just learn to say "please," Dad!

Cleopatra's father was Pharaoh Ptolemy XII of Egypt. His family was originally from Greece, but they had ruled Egypt for more than two hundred years.

What do you know about Egyptian culture, Dad?

Not a lot, Cleo.

Cleo spoke seven languages.

Cleopatra was really smart and became the first of her family to speak Egyptian. Her father adored her and taught her all he knew about ruling Egypt.

OK, so Dad's dead and I'll do the ruling.

Not for long, sister!

When Cleopatra was eighteen years old, she and her younger brother, ten-year-old Ptolemy XIII, inherited their father's throne.

You're a little squirt. You know nothing about ruling!

I'm a boy, so I do the ruling.

Her little brother was no real match for her cunning and ambition!

In Egypt, women were supposed to come second to men, but Cleopatra didn't like that idea. She wanted to be the sole ruler of Egypt.

Now you're out, and I'm in.

Not for long, brother!

As he grew older, her brother Ptolemy objected to this and finally threw Cleopatra out of the palace so he could rule alone.

How can you resist me?

I can't.

If Caesar hadn't loved Cleo, he might have conquered Egypt.

Soon after, Julius Caesar, the Roman leader, arrived in Egypt. Cleopatra hid inside a rug and had herself delivered to him. He was captivated!

Never mess with your sister!

Caesar helped Cleopatra raise an army against Ptolemy. He was no match for the ambitious pair and died at the Battle of the Nile.

Help, Dot. I've shrunk!

It's book magic, Abe.

Do you think Cleo loved Caesar?

Probably not!

Cleopatra was queen of Egypt again! She was very popular and helped Egypt become a rich and successful country.

Cleopatra and Caesar had a son they nicknamed Caesarion, but Caesar refused to make him his heir, naming his grandnephew Octavian instead.

In 44 BCE, Caesar was murdered, and Cleopatra feared Octavian would invade Egypt.

To protect his future, Cleopatra made Caesarion her coruler, but she kept the real power herself.

Then she persuaded Mark Antony, one of Rome's new leaders, to join forces with her.

Mark Antony fell deeply in love with Cleopatra. The pair challenged Octavian to a battle at sea in 31 BCE, but their heavy ships were no match for the Roman vessels, and Octavian defeated them.

Antony and Cleopatra fled to Egypt, where Antony killed himself after hearing the false news of Cleopatra's death. Heartbroken, Cleopatra dressed in her finest clothes and then allowed a poisonous asp to bite her, so that she would die too.

After Cleopatra's death, Octavian made Egypt part of the Roman Empire. So, although her son Caesarion may have held nominal power for a few days before Octavian had him executed, Cleopatra was the last-ever true pharaoh of Egypt.

Caesarion means "little Caesar."

Cleo dressed as the goddess Isis to capture Antony's heart!

Cleo feared becoming Octavian's prisoner.

Cleo was only thirty-nine years old when she died.

*Boudicca* is derived from a Celtic word for "victory."

# Boudicca
## Warrior Queen of the Iceni
### C. 25–61 CE

"Stop fighting, Boudicca, and feed the chickens!"

"Ouch!"

"She's a warrior through and through!"

Boudicca was born in southeast Britain. She lived with her parents until she was seven, when they died.

Boudicca was a Celt. Celts lived in Britain before the Romans arrived.

"We'll teach you how to weave."

Luckily, Boudicca was adopted by another family.

"I'm a warrior, not a weaver!"

"So I see!"

They sent her to warrior school, where she learned to fight.

She was fearless and had fierce eyes that made enemies tremble!

She always seemed destined for greatness.

"I think I've taught you all I can."

Boudicca grew to be very tall and had flowing red hair.

"My little wildcat!"

She married Prasutagus, king of the Iceni tribe of eastern England.

"I think they take after you, Boudi."

They had two daughters, and life was good.

Not wise to steal from a warrior queen!

"Last week they took the harvest. This week it's the chickens!"

"Now what'll I have to eat?"

"Roman hens!"

At the time, Britain was under Roman power. They let Prasutagus rule his kingdom but charged taxes.

"Those Romans have to go!"

In 60 CE, Prasutagus died, and the Romans seized his wealth, leaving his family with nothing!

"I thought all warriors were men!"

"Well, you were wrong!"

"Boudicca is scarily fierce!"

The Iceni people rebelled, but the Romans were too strong for them. Some Iceni had their homes burned to the ground, and others were enslaved. Boudicca and her daughters were tortured.

Boudicca was outraged! She rallied other tribes, and together they captured three Roman cities. Then they were attacked by the Roman governor and his army of ten thousand men. Boudicca was leading about one hundred thousand men, so it seemed like she would win, but her men weren't trained, and they were already tired and hungry after their recent battles. Boudicca's army was defeated. Boudicca and her daughters poisoned themselves to avoid being captured. Her rebellion had not succeeded in chasing the Romans from Britain, but it did eventually lead to all Celtic tribes' getting a fairer deal from the Romans. Boudicca never let the Romans conquer her, and she became a symbol to some freedom fighters.

# Joan of Arc

## Teenage Warrior
### C. 1412–1431

*"I would rather die than do something which I know to be a sin, or to be against God's will."*

The struggle between France and England from 1337 to 1453 is called the Hundred Years' War.

In 1412, when Joan was born in the French village of Domrémy, much of France was under English rule. When Joan was nine years old, her village was raided by English soldiers.

Joan often heard voices through the notes of the church bells.

Joan was a quiet, gentle child. She didn't go to school but instead worked on her father's farm.

She was very religious and loved going to church, even when her friends wanted her to play!

Joan liked to take the bell ringer little presents.

When Joan was thirteen years old, she began to hear voices and see visions of saints and angels. Joan grew to love and trust the voices.

When Joan was sixteen, the Archangel Michael, Saint Catherine, and Saint Margaret told Joan to drive the English out of France. Joan believed it was God's will.

Because Joan believed the voices came from God, she felt bound to obey them.

Dressed as a soldier, Joan went to the French ruler, the Dauphin Charles. He laughed at her! But his soldiers continued losing to the English.

Joan was eventually given a suit of armor and command of the French army. Awed by their leader, the soldiers went into battle with renewed hope.

Led by Joan, the French army drove the English from the city of Orléans and then from smaller towns close by.

Afterward they marched to Reims, where Charles was crowned king of France! Joan was now ready to go home, but the king ordered her to fight on.

During a battle at Compiègne, Joan was captured by the French traitor the Duke of Burgundy. Ransomed to the English, she was imprisoned.

In 1431, after an unfair trial, Joan was found guilty of heresy. She was burned in the marketplace at Rouen at the age of nineteen. King Charles did not lift a finger to rescue the girl who had saved France from the English and won his crown for him! Today the French see Joan of Arc as a national hero.

Joan led her men into battle, brandishing her banner instead of a sword.

She was wounded several times in battle, but she always fought on.

Joan could get very angry if her soldiers behaved badly or skipped church.

Pope Benedict XV declared Joan a saint in 1920.

*"There shall be but one mistress here, and no master."*

# Elizabeth I

Queen of England, Wales & Ireland

1533–1603

A beautiful daughter!

Take her away. I need a son!

Elizabeth I was born in London on September 7, 1533. Her dad, Henry VIII, was not pleased! He wanted a son to inherit his crown.

Dad'll be turning in his grave!

Elizabeth was crowned in 1558 when her half sister Mary died.

My people are my children.

England is my husband.

Parliament wanted Elizabeth to marry, but she politely refused.

If I marry, my husband will get to rule instead of me!

Elizabeth was very clever and wanted to rule the country herself.

Shall we talk in English, French, Italian, Spanish, Greek, or Latin?

Um . . .

I'm fast and furious!

Knock, knock. Who's there?

Sleep tomorrow night, if you must!

Elizabeth spoke six languages. She loved riding, playing music, writing poetry, dancing, flirting, and making jokes. She also worked extremely hard, often keeping her ministers up all night!

Dolt!

Idiot!

Cod's head!

Puh!

Elizabeth was not perfect. She was moody and sometimes spat at or beat servants who displeased her.

Three cheers for good Queen Bess!

We are charmed to meet you!

However, in public, Elizabeth was always gracious. She dressed to impress her people and they loved her.

Inheriting a crown doesn't make you great!

It's what you do with it that counts!

Elizabeth increased literacy . . .

helped the poor . . .

Luckily, Elizabeth had built up her father's depleted navy.

Elizabeth employed spies to warn her of impending attacks!

Elizabeth tried hard to avoid wars, but it was impossible. She was a Protestant, and some people wanted a Catholic on the throne. Mary Queen of Scots, who was a Catholic, spent nineteen years plotting against her, and in 1588, the Catholic king of Spain sent a fleet of ships called the Armada to invade England. Aided by a storm, Elizabeth's navy triumphed! Elizabeth rode through the streets in celebration.

Her naval commanders finished their bowling games before attacking the Spanish.

Not bad for a girl, huh, Daddy?

Elizabeth hated getting old. She had all the mirrors removed from her palaces.

Elizabeth didn't have children, so she was the last monarch of the Tudor dynasty. When she died in 1603, the crown passed to King James VI of Scotland, uniting England and Scotland. Elizabeth I had inherited a troubled nation but made it so strong and prosperous that her reign became known as "The Golden Age."

proved that women were amazing . . .

expanded trade . . .

and introduced the first flush toilets!

Now, that really did change the world!

# Mary Wollstonecraft

## Author & Feminist
### 1759–1797

*"The divine right of husbands, like the divine right of kings, may, it is hoped, in this enlightened age, be contested without danger."*

Hurry and pack! We're moving.

Can I help, Mother?

No, Mary, you're just a nuisance!

Mary was born in London on April 27, 1759. Her childhood was miserable — her mother disliked her, and her father was a bully. He also kept moving his family to avoid paying his debts.

*Mary tried to help and protect her mother.*

Girls and boys are equal, so we should learn the same.

Don't be silly, dear.

Mary was smart and longed to learn history and Latin like her brothers, but girls were taught only needlework and simple arithmetic.

*In Mary's time, few women received the same education as men.*

These are the books you should read.

Without you I would be quite ignorant.

When Mary was fifteen, she was befriended by her intellectual neighbors, Mr. and Mrs. Clare, who let her use their library.

And who will look after me?

Not me, Mama. I have a life to live.

Mary wanted to be independent and left home at nineteen to be a "lady's companion." Later, she opened a school with her best friend, Fanny.

*Women were expected to marry or stay at home.*

Will you ever marry, Mary, dear?

Not unless we live as equals.

Fanny eventually married, but Mary didn't believe in marriage. She wanted to stay single and earn her own living.

I feel so alone now.

Sadly, Fanny became ill after the birth of her first child and died. Mary, who had few like-minded friends, was heartbroken.

*Mary was like a bird — she wanted to fly free!*

You cannot stay in this miserable marriage.

But I'll starve without a husband to provide for me.

After rescuing her sister from a violent marriage, Mary had to give up her school, but she was determined to remain independent.

Even I know girls and boys are equal!

In Mary's time, many boys didn't realize that.

Equality for all people!

Indeed!

I'm trained for nothing. Maybe one of our brothers will care for me.

I'm going to be independent and an inspiration to other women!

Mary decided to support herself as an author, which was very brave, as few women earned an income from writing at this time.

You're very brave, employing a woman.

They have brains too.

That's so radical!

But true!

Mary worked for a publisher and met many freethinkers like herself, including the poets William Wordsworth and William Blake.

Many people were shocked by Mary's writings.

In the first book, I argue that kings and queens shouldn't exist, and that people should have equal opportunities.

In the second, I argue that women are as intelligent as men and should be given the same education.

Mary wrote several books and political pamphlets. The two most famous were *A Vindication of the Rights of Men* and *A Vindication of the Rights of Woman*.

I can't marry you, but I'll love you and our daughter.

Society will shun you.

In 1792, drawn by the French Revolution, Mary went to Paris. She fell in love with an American, Gilbert Imlay, and they had a daughter, Fanny.

In France, Mary felt less restricted and more able to be herself.

I think she's going to be a writer and freethinker like me!

Can't you send her back?

Then we should call her Mary, after you!

When the relationship collapsed, Mary returned to London with Fanny, and she eventually married the philosopher and writer William Godwin. Their marriage was unconventional for the time — William respected Mary's right to work, and he shared the household duties with her. They had a daughter, but, tragically, Mary died eleven days after giving birth. She was only thirty-eight. Mary lived during a period when women's voices were rarely listened to, but she had made herself heard! She is now seen as one of the founders of feminism, and her books went on to inspire women to fight for the right to vote.

Little Mary grew up and wrote *Frankenstein*. She married the poet Percy Bysshe Shelley.

Feminists want equal rights for women and men.

So, who's next?

A writer who didn't even get to put her name on her novels.

No way!

You better believe it!

# Jane Austen

## Novelist
### 1775–1817

*"Know your own happiness."*

Much of what we know about Jane's childhood comes from her letters. Unfortunately her sister destroyed many of them.

Jane was born in Hampshire, England, on December 16, 1775, to George and Cassandra Austen. She was the seventh of eight children—six boys and two girls.

Jane's father was intelligent, and her mother was shrewd.

Her father was a clergyman who also tutored young boys.

Jane was a lively little girl and very close to her sister, Cassandra.

For a while they went to boarding school together.

At this time, girls were not encouraged to read novels!

Back at home, Jane was determined to educate herself.

She read all the books in her father's library.

She also listened when he taught his pupils!

Jane often read her stories aloud to her family.

From an early age, Jane had a passion for writing.

She wrote poems, stories, and plays for her family to act out.

Jane had a talent for writing about people in everyday situations.

Jane wrote *Sense and Sensibility*, *Pride and Prejudice*, and *Northanger Abbey* by the age of twenty-three!

What were her other books called?

*Mansfield Park*, *Emma*, and *Persuasion*.

Jane often wrote about love but never married. She had a short romance with Tom Lefroy, a young man from Ireland, but he never proposed.

When she was twenty-seven, Jane accepted an offer of marriage from a rich landowner. But the very next morning she changed her mind!

Jane never stopped writing. In 1797 her father sent an early version of her novel *Pride and Prejudice* to a publisher, but it was rejected.

Then, in 1803, her brother Henry sent an early version of *Northanger Abbey* to a publisher. He said he would publish it but never did!

When Jane's father died, Jane and her sister and mother moved to a cottage on their brother's estate. And in 1811, her first book — *Sense and Sensibility* — was published! Jane published three more during her lifetime, all anonymously. It wasn't considered "proper" for women to have jobs — or even to have their own opinions! When Jane died at age forty-one, Henry revealed that she had written the books. Jane's books were very popular during her lifetime, and they're even more popular now. She is one of the world's best-loved novelists.

Jane once wrote to her niece telling her not to marry a man she didn't love.

Scary gothic novels were fashionable at the time.

I'm glad she had her sister for company.

Jane is believed to have coined more than forty new terms, including doorbell, sponge cake, and dinner party.

# Florence Nightingale

## Nursing Pioneer
### 1820–1910

*"I attribute my success to this: I never gave or took an excuse."*

In Victorian England, nursing was not considered a respectable profession but rather work for the uneducated.

From an early age, Florence had a passion for nursing. She was born into a large, wealthy family, so she had plenty of relations to practice on — as well as all her dolls!

Florence was very smart and excellent at math.

After a visit to a local hospital, which was squalid and uncaring — as most hospitals were at that time — Florence decided to become a professional nurse.

Her parents did not believe that respectable young women should become nurses, but they finally allowed her to go to Germany for training.

Fortunately, her dad believed in educating girls!

Then, in March 1854, Britain and France joined the Ottoman Empire in the Crimean War against Russia. British soldiers were rushed into battle.

Florence wanted to help. So the minister of war asked her to take a team of thirty-eight nurses to the army hospital in Scutari, Turkey.

Dr. Hall was worried Florence would send bad reports back to England.

When Florence arrived, Dr. Hall, who was in charge, tried to drive her away. He didn't want her team to see the terrible conditions he'd permitted.

Florence wasn't going anywhere! She and her nurses set about scrubbing the filthy wards, exterminating the rats, and making the soldiers more comfortable.

Florence and her nurses also took over the kitchens so the soldiers would have warm and nourishing food.

When winter came and the men had no suitable clothing, Florence brought them warm clothes and blankets.

Florence met Mary Seacole, another famous nurse working in the Crimean War.

Dr. Hall continued to make Florence's life difficult, but the other doctors were grateful for her care and the improvement in their patients.

The soldiers loved Florence, and many of them owed their lives to her. They called her "the Lady with the Lamp" because of her late-night ward rounds.

Florence became known as "the Angel of the Crimea."

In Victorian times, only the rich had access to health care.

At the end of the war, Florence returned home a hero. Queen Victoria presented her with a gold brooch. Florence used her fame to help improve nursing and sanitation for all. She opened a school for nurses and worked until her death at age ninety, writing and collecting statistics to prove the importance of hygiene and skilled nurses in preventing the spread of disease. Through her passion, intelligence, and determination, Florence changed the face of health care for many people, both in England and abroad.

Florence used her own money to send trained nurses into workhouses.

Marie has many firsts to her name!

Marie was the first woman to receive a PhD from a French university . . .

the first woman to be employed as a professor at the University of Paris . . .

and the first woman to win a Nobel Prize— one of the most prestigious prizes in the world!

Albert Einstein was a great admirer of Marie.

# MARIE CURIE

## Physicist & Chemist
### 1867–1934

*"I was taught that the way of progress was neither swift nor easy."*

We love our children too!

Marie was born in Warsaw, Poland, and was the youngest of five children. She was a bright child. Her parents were both teachers and loved poetry, books, and learning.

We'll look after you, Papa.

When Marie was just ten years old, her mother died of tuberculosis.

"Nothing in life is to be feared, Papa. It is only to be understood."

Sad as she was, Marie continued to do brilliantly at school.

You take my classes today, Marie.

Oh, no, Papa, I'm too little!

Like her father, she was particularly good at math and physics.

One day women will be able to attend.

I hope you're right.

But Marie was not able to attend the men-only university in Warsaw, so she and her sister Bronya joined a secret group that held classes for women.

You go first — you're the eldest.

Can't you swap? She looks more fun!

Marie also worked as a governess, to pay for Bronya to study as a doctor in Paris.

Mon Dieu, who's going to pick Marie up today?

She's whiter than a boiled egg!

Women students!

When Bronya qualified, she invited Marie to live with her and study in Paris too. Marie had very little money and sometimes fainted from hunger. But she still completed degrees in physics and math!

What would you do if you had Marie's brains?

Design shoes that help you do a double backflip!

How's that going to help your fellow humans?

In 1894, Marie met and fell in love with Pierre Curie, a fellow physicist. The couple married and had two children, Irène and Ève.

Marie and Pierre started working together in a drafty shed, researching radioactivity — radiation or particles given off by certain elements.

They discovered two new elements: polonium and radium. Tragically, in 1906 Pierre was killed in a carriage accident. Marie carried on their work, winning a second Nobel Prize, this one in Chemistry.

During World War I, Marie created X-ray machines for ambulances. She and her daughter Irène drove one of these "Little Curies" to the front lines.

Marie had taken over Pierre's teaching post at Sorbonne University in Paris, becoming the first female professor there. After the war, she gave lectures around the world, famous as the first person to win the Nobel Prize twice! Her discoveries led to radiation being used to treat diseases such as cancer and inspired many other scientists.

Marie kept a sample of glowing radium next to her bed as a nightlight . . .

she didn't realize the dangers of overexposure to radiation.

Marie named polonium in honor of her homeland, Poland.

Marie tried to donate her gold Nobel Prize medals to the war effort.

Marie's eldest daughter also won the Nobel Prize for Chemistry.

# Eleanor Roosevelt

## Human Rights Activist
### 1884–1962

*"You must do the things you think you cannot do."*

*Roosevelt means "rose field" in Dutch.*

*Eleanor was born twenty years after the abolition of slavery in America.*

*But there was still much social, political, and racial inequality.*

*Eleanor had a passion for field hockey at school.*

Eleanor Roosevelt was born in New York on October 11, 1884, into a wealthy but rather unhappy and distant family.

Eleanor's father, Elliott, suffered from depression, which her mother found hard to cope with.

Eleanor tried to comfort her mother, but her mother was often unkind and found no comfort in Eleanor.

When Eleanor was eight, her mother died, and Eleanor grew very close to her father. She would count the minutes until he returned from work.

Eleanor was heartbroken when, several months after her mother's death, her father died too. Eleanor went to live with her grandmother, Mary Hall.

Eleanor did not feel at home at her grandmother's, but luckily, when she was fifteen, her grandmother sent her to school in England. Eleanor blossomed — she made friends, traveled widely, and learned to be confident, independent, and articulate. She stayed in England for three happy years.

Eleanor said we should fight for people's freedoms every day!

Well, she certainly did that — exhausting!

And she went flying with Amelia Earhart and applied for her own pilot's license.

I'm going to join the Junior League to help people who are less privileged than me.

We'll join you. We're sick of parties!

When Eleanor returned to New York, she was expected to go to parties and find a husband. But Eleanor was more interested in helping poorer people.

Life is what you make of it, children!

Yes, Mama!

Eleanor married her cousin Franklin Roosevelt, who also wanted to improve life for less privileged people. They had six children, one of whom died as a baby.

Franklin called Eleanor "Babs."

WHITE SEATING

We can't arrest her — she's far too important.

RESTROOMS

WHITE

COLORED

COLORED SEATING

And then, in 1933, Franklin became president of the United States of America! Eleanor supported him as First Lady but continued her fight for social justice. In 1938, at a Human Welfare conference in Birmingham, Alabama, Eleanor defied the state's segregation laws. When ordered to move out of the "Colored Seating" and into the "White Seating," Eleanor placed her chair exactly halfway between the two areas!

Eleanor's uncle was Theodore Roosevelt, who had been the twenty-sixth president of the United States.

No one served as First Lady longer — 12 years!

## THE UNIVERSAL DECLARATION OF HUMAN RIGHTS

Adopted by the General Assembly of the United Nations in 1948, the Universal Declaration states basic rights and fundamental freedoms to which all human beings are entitled.

ALL HUMAN BEINGS ARE BORN FREE AND EQUAL.

EVERYONE IS ENTITLED TO THESE RIGHTS NO MATTER THEIR RACE, RELIGION, OR NATIONALITY.

EVERYONE HAS THE RIGHT TO LIFE, LIBERTY, AND SECURITY.

Pretty good for a plain and solemn child!

Eleanor wrote a newspaper column called "My Day," and she also wrote twenty-seven books!

After Franklin died in 1945, Eleanor represented the USA at the United Nations and helped draft the Universal Declaration of Human Rights. She was repeatedly voted America's "Most Admired Woman of the Year" for her commitment to the rights of all people, and she was active and influential for the rest of her life.

Who's Amelia whatsit?

Ah, I think you are going to like her.

Could she do double backflips?

Yes, but in an airplane!

# AMELIA EARHART

Pilot

1897–1937

*"Women must try to do things as men have tried."*

*I won't wear stinky dresses or play with soppy dolls, so woof to you!*

When Amelia Earhart was born in Atchison, Kansas, on July 24, 1897, little girls were expected to wear pretty dresses and play quietly with dolls, but Amelia never liked to do either.

*I'm flying!*

*The Bogie's behind you!*

*It's a madhouse!*

Amelia, her sister, Grace Muriel, and their dog, James Ferocious, all liked adventure. Ferocious chased strangers while the girls built a roller coaster, tobogganed, cycled, and played a scary make-believe game called Bogie!

*Boring. Our roller coaster's loads more fun!*

In 1909, the Wright brothers circled the Statue of Liberty while flying one of the first airplanes. Amelia was unimpressed with the rickety planes of the time.

*You're a pilot at heart!*

*I swear that plane spoke to me.*

But ten years later, Amelia was at a stunt-flying exhibition when a pilot nosedived toward her. Amelia was hooked on planes from that moment!

*There are times when you have to conform. What do you think?*

*Grrrr!*

*Nurse!*

*Nurse!*

*Nurse!*

*Hurry up, nurse.*

*Nurse!*

*Nurse!*

During World War I, while visiting family in Canada, Amelia met wounded soldiers and immediately left school to become a nurse's aide. Then, in 1920, a pilot took her on her first flight, and Amelia knew she had to learn to fly herself.

*I think Amelia could definitely do double backflips!*

*Yeah, she was seriously cool.*

*If it weren't for women like her, men might own the sky.*

In ancient times, people tried to fly with wings made of feathers.

Yeah, they'd jump off towers and crash to the ground!

In 1783, there were successful hot-air balloon flights.

But there were no really successful winged flights until the Wright brothers.

24

Amelia started to save money for flying lessons. By 1922, she had her first plane and set her first women's record by flying to an altitude of 14,000 feet.

On June 17, 1928, Amelia became the first woman to fly across the Atlantic. She and her crew returned to New York to a ticker-tape parade.

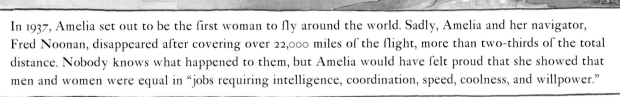

In 1937, Amelia set out to be the first woman to fly around the world. Sadly, Amelia and her navigator, Fred Noonan, disappeared after covering over 22,000 miles of the flight, more than two-thirds of the total distance. Nobody knows what happened to them, but Amelia would have felt proud that she showed that men and women were equal in "jobs requiring intelligence, coordination, speed, coolness, and willpower."

The first African-American woman to fly was Bessie Coleman in 1922.

Bessie was a daredevil, just like Amelia!

Yes, they both liked to challenge the traditional role of women.

I think I'll challenge the role of birds and start walking!

Watch out for cats, then!

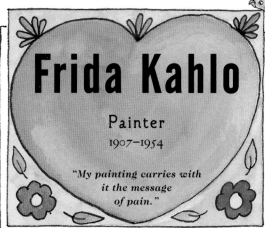

# Frida Kahlo

## Painter
### 1907–1954

*"My painting carries with it the message of pain."*

Frida lived and died in the Blue House.

Frida Kahlo was born in Coyoacán, Mexico, on July 6, 1907. She had five sisters and lived in a house called the Blue House with her German father and her Spanish-Mexican mother.

Frida's father encouraged her to get an education.

You must swim, play football, and wrestle. Then your leg will get strong!

When Frida was six years old, she caught a disease called polio that left her right leg damaged for life.

Then, when Frida was eighteen, she suffered life-changing injuries in a bus accident.

Her mother wanted her to learn to cook and get married!

You can paint.

Frida had to stay in bed for months. Her parents encouraged her to take up painting. They built her a special easel so that she could paint while lying on her back. She painted herself and her school friends.

Frida's self-portraits were always honest.

"I paint my own reality."

Frida was never really strong again. She gave up her dream of becoming a doctor but continued to paint. Frida started to paint self-portraits that reflected the pain caused by her accident and were influenced by Mexican folk art.

Do you get the feeling you're inside a Frida Kahlo painting?

Yes. Isn't it a good adventure?

It's very colorful, but prickly too.

**We must create a classless world!**

Frida supported the Mexican revolutionaries who wanted political change. She was never afraid to attend rallies and spoke out against social injustice.

**"I love you more than my own skin."**

In 1929, Frida married Diego Rivera, a famous muralist. They went to live in America, and Frida started to exhibit her work. It received a mixed reception.

**Diego was by far the worst accident in my life!**

The couple eventually returned to Mexico, but they had a very difficult relationship and lived separately for long periods.

**I paint to escape.**

Frida's work was getting more recognition, but her health was getting worse. In 1950 she spent nine months in a hospital, but she never stopped painting.

**"Feet, what do I need you for when I have wings to fly?"**

**I like your paintings.**

In 1953 she had her first solo exhibition in Mexico. She was very ill, so she arrived by ambulance and then held court from a four-poster bed in the gallery!

**"I hope the exit is joyful and I hope never to return."**

Frida Kahlo died on July 13, 1954, just after her forty-seventh birthday. Even though she struggled with pain and unhappiness throughout her life, Frida remained strong, determined, and honest. We can still see this today in the colorful and beautiful paintings that she left behind to inspire us.

Diego and Frida got divorced and then remarried.

Frida adapted native Mexican fashion to hide her scars.

Frida went on her last protest march ten days before her death.

Frida is still seen by many as an icon of female creativity.

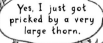
**Yes, I just got pricked by a very large thorn.**

**Frida painted life's thorns and roses!**

**She was a free-flying spirit!**

# Anne Frank

### Writer
### 1929–1945

*"Whoever is happy will make others happy too."*

In June 1929, in Frankfurt, Germany, a Jewish woman named Edith Frank gave birth to a baby she called Anne. Edith, her husband, Otto, and their first daughter, Margot, were all delighted.

Otto and Edith Frank encouraged both of their daughters to read.

But in 1933, Adolf Hitler, of the Nazi party, became leader of Germany. Hitler persecuted Jewish people, so the Franks moved to Amsterdam, in the Netherlands.

Hitler tried to turn everyone against Jews.

Anne was a bright, playful four-year-old and soon learned to speak Dutch. Both she and Margot loved their new schools.

Then, in 1939, World War II began. A year later, Germany invaded the Netherlands. Life became increasingly difficult for Jewish people.

Jews had to wear the yellow Star of David.

Anne and Margot had to leave the schools they loved and move to a Jewish school. Otto had to hand over his business to non-Jewish friends.

The family tried to live normally, celebrating special occasions. On Anne's thirteenth birthday, they gave her a diary, and she began to write about life under the Nazis.

Jews couldn't use public transportation or even sit on public benches.

Meanwhile, Otto had prepared a hideout behind a bookcase at his office. Soon after Anne's birthday, fearing arrest, the family moved in.

Walking down the street must have been so scary!

In order not to arouse suspicion when they moved in, the family had to wear their clothes in layers and just fill a satchel with precious possessions. Anne took her new diary!

The hideout was very small and cramped, especially once another couple, the van Pels, moved in with their son, Peter, and their friend, a dentist named Fritz Pfeffer. Forced to remain quiet and indoors, Anne comforted herself by sharing all her teenage thoughts and secrets with her diary. The Franks had good friends outside who supplied them with food, books, and other provisions, but after two years, they were discovered by the Nazis.

Otto was the only one of the family to survive the concentration camp.

In August 1944, the Nazis stormed into the secret hideout and sent everyone to prison camps. Sadly, Anne died of an illness called typhus in early 1945. She was just fifteen years old. Since then, millions of people have read her diary, which shows the strength of the human spirit in the midst of unimaginable horror.

After the war he found Anne's diary and published it.

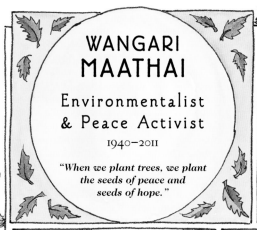

# WANGARI MAATHAI

### Environmentalist & Peace Activist

#### 1940–2011

*"When we plant trees, we plant the seeds of peace and seeds of hope."*

In April 1940, a girl named Wangari was born in a small village in Nyeri, Kenya. The village was shaded from the hot African sun by beautiful trees. Wangari grew up listening to the chatter of the birds and animals that shared their forest.

Wangari's father was a farmer.

Good job, Wangari.

From an early age, Wangari enjoyed helping her mother grow and harvest their food.

She also fetched water and caught fish from a nearby stream that flowed cool and clear.

Then Wangari and her mother would gather firewood and cook together. There was always plenty for all.

Wangari loved the color of the red Kenyan soil.

Your ancestors' spirits rest in the shade of this tree.

Are you there, great-grandfather?

When her work was done, Wangari loved to lie in the shade of the trees and listen to her mother's tales about their ancestors.

Girls don't go to school!

Wangari will go!

You heard your mother.

When Wangari was eight years old, her parents sent her to school. She worked very hard, and in 1960 she won a scholarship to study in the US.

When Wangari was a child, few Kenyan girls went to school.

Where are the trees, the shade, the animals, the birdsong?

The loggers came and cut down the trees.

The animals and birds have lost their homes.

Crops won't grow.

I'm hungry.

In America, Wangari was awarded a degree in biology, the science of living things. But when she returned home in 1966, Wangari found that many of the living things in Kenya had vanished. Loggers and farmers had cut down millions of trees, so the land had become barren. Children were hungry, and women had to walk miles for water and firewood.

No trees means no birds—meet the desert rats.

One person can make a BIG difference!

I'm going to collect a bag of acorns and plant them.

The women are planting trees so the birds will soon be back!

*Mama Miti* means "mother of trees" in Swahili.

In 1971, Wangari became the first woman from East and Central Africa to earn a doctorate.

Wangari knew that without trees, land becomes desert and crops and animals are unable to thrive. She also realized that as food and water became scarcer, people would become poorer and start fighting over the small amount that remained. So Wangari talked to women all over Kenya. She showed them how to plant and tend to trees. The women could earn some money for keeping the trees alive and could sell the firewood they didn't need. Thousands of women took up Wangari's challenge, and what became known as the Green Belt Movement began as little saplings were nurtured all across the land.

On World Environment Day in 1977, Wangari launched her movement by planting seven trees in a Nairobi park.

Wangari was also a political activist, calling for democracy and freedom of expression.

In 2004, Wangari became the first environmentalist and African woman to be awarded the Nobel Peace Prize for her contribution to "sustainable development, democracy, and peace." In Kenya the tree is a symbol of peace, so to celebrate her prize, Wangari planted a Nandi flame tree at the base of Mount Kenya. The Green Belt Movement has planted more than fifty million trees and increased the income and independence of countless women. Children in Kenya can once again sit in the shade of a tree and listen to tales of their ancestors.

# Mae C. Jemison

## The First African-American Woman in Space

### born 1956

*"Never be limited by other people's limited imaginations."*

The first woman in space was Soviet cosmonaut Valentina Tereshkova, in 1963.

About 550 people have flown in space. About 60 of them were women.

In space, a sneeze can send you flying backward!

Zero gravity makes a candle flame perfectly round.

Mae Jemison spent her childhood in Chicago and, even when she was in kindergarten, dreamed of becoming a scientist.

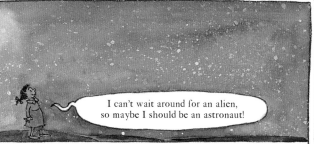

Mae was a stargazer, and she wouldn't let anyone limit her dreams. She never doubted that she would be one of the first American women astronauts.

But Mae also had other ambitions. She wanted to be a dancer and a doctor! Her mother persuaded her to go to medical school and dance in her spare time.

In 1981, Mae graduated from Cornell Medical College and joined a volunteer group called the Peace Corps. She worked as a doctor in Liberia and Sierra Leone.

After seeing Sally Ride become the first American woman in space, Mae applied to the NASA space program. Finally, in 1987, she was accepted!

**THINGS SPACE SCIENTISTS STUDY:**
- Growing vegetables under weightless conditions
- How to make better medicine
- Bone density
- Space sickness

Mae was the first African-American woman admitted into the astronaut training program. After a year of training, she earned the title Science Mission Specialist. This meant that Mae was able to conduct scientific experiments, such as about the effects of weightlessness (or zero gravity) on space shuttle crews.

The shuttle launches like a rocket, orbits like a spacecraft, and lands like a plane.

A space shuttle's external tank is just taller than the Statue of Liberty.

"I belong here as much as any speck of stardust."

EXTERNAL TANK

SOLID ROCKET BOOSTER

The crew lives here!

Usually space suits are worn during takeoff and landing only, to protect the astronaut if there is a problem with the air in the shuttle. There is no air in space, so space suits carry a supply. Mae's was orange so she could easily be spotted by rescuers if she had to parachute from the spacecraft.

ORBITER: the part that travels to space and back

**READY FOR LAUNCH**

**MAE IN HER SPACE SUIT**

In space, water doesn't bubble when it boils, and your face swells up.

In space, astronauts' legs get thinner — they develop bird legs!

Fruit flies, mice, monkeys, chimpanzees, guinea pigs, rabbits, frogs, reptiles, and dogs have all gone on space missions!

Another space heroine, Katherine Johnson (born 1918), joined NASA in the 1950s as a "computer" — a mathematician. She helped put the first person on the Moon!

Mae flew her space mission from September 12 to 20, 1992, on the shuttle *Endeavour*. She took a poster from a dance theater along with art objects from West African countries on her space mission to symbolize that space belongs to all nations and all peoples. When Mae looked down from space on Chicago, she imagined the little girl down there that she used to be and thought that little girl would be "tickled" to see Mae the astronaut! Once back on Earth, Mae decided to leave NASA to develop technology that can help people all over the world in their daily lives. Mae also opened a summer camp for budding young scientists, and she encourages everyone to get involved with space exploration, whatever their race, gender, or background.

Yes, it looks like an airplane toilet!

I love it when people follow their dreams.

Especially when they catch them!

# Cathy Freeman

## Olympic Hero
### born 1973

"I enjoy being a woman!"

Look, Mama, these feet are born to run!

Never mind running — are you talking already?

Cathy was born in February 1973 in Queensland, Australia, to Aboriginal parents. Aboriginal Australians are the country's indigenous people, and they have often been oppressed by European settlers.

Cathy, please just walk!

I can't; I'm a runner!

"It all comes down to having the confidence to be who you are!"

That's just what I tell my little Roo!

Cathy's full name is Catherine Astrid Salome Freeman.

From a young age, Cathy knew she wanted to be a runner and showed great talent, but her family had no money for a professional trainer.

But Cathy was very determined, and she was just eight years old when she won her first gold medal, at a school athletics competition.

Go, girl!

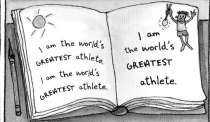

I am the world's GREATEST athlete. I am the world's GREATEST athlete.

I am the world's GREATEST athlete.

Now I'll get the training I need to win an Olympic gold!

Cathy's stepfather always believed she'd win an Olympic gold medal!

Cathy's stepfather helped her train. She ran barefoot around and around a grass track.

Her mother encouraged her to write "I am the world's greatest athlete" over and over again.

When she was thirteen, Cathy became one of a very few Aboriginal children to win a scholarship to boarding school.

That's a public proclamation of Aboriginal rights.

Tut-tut!

Shocking!

Go, Cathy!

Quite right!

She's brave! Go, Cathy, go!

A teacher bought Cathy her first running shoes.

At just sixteen years old, Cathy won a gold medal at the 1990 Commonwealth Games in the 100-meter relay. Then, in 1994, Cathy won individual gold medals in the 200- and 400-meter races. She ran her lap of honor waving both the Australian flag and the Aboriginal flag, shocking some people but delighting others.

Cathy just followed her dream.

She was amazing!

Do you think she's got the longest and the fastest legs ever?!

Want to hear me laugh . . . heeeheeeheee!

The first Aboriginal Australian to win an Olympic medal was Samantha Riley in 1992.

In 1996, Cathy won a silver medal at the Olympics in the 400-meter race.

In 1990, Cathy was chosen as the Young Australian of the Year . . .

and in 1998, she was named Australian of the Year!

Cathy has a tattoo that reads: "Cos I'm Free."

In 2000, when the Olympics were held in Sydney, Australia, Cathy was chosen to light the Olympic flame. Then, to the delight of her home crowd, Cathy went on to win a gold medal in the 400-meter race. This time when Cathy waved both the Aboriginal flag and the Australian flag, the crowd cheered wildly! Cathy Freeman may not have been the first Aboriginal Australian to win an Olympic medal, but by sharing her pride in her roots, she is helping to unite a nation and serves as a symbol of hope for the Aboriginal people. Cathy is now retired from racing, but she continues to fight for the rights of Aboriginal Australians.

Probably, but I think mine might grow longer!

You must be joking! Want to hear about my favorite hero?

Is your hero a scientist, writer, or adventurer?

Let's see!

# MALALA YOUSAFZAI

## Children's & Women's Rights Activist

born 1997

*"I am stronger than fear!"*

Malala is a Pashtun. Pashtuns are people from Pakistan and Afghanistan.

The Taliban are followers of Islam, but they have more extreme beliefs than most Muslims.

Malala wrote her blog under the name Gul Makai, a heroine from a Pashtun folktale.

The Taliban banned many things, like makeup, kite flying, music, and films.

*Pakistan* means "land of the pure" in Urdu and Persian.

Malala was born on July 12, 1997, in the beautiful Swat Valley of Pakistan. When she was little, it was a safe place where girls and boys ran free, flying kites and playing in the streets.

There is so much to learn, and I want to learn it all.

Malala went to a school started by her father, Ziauddin. School meant everything to Malala!

"How dare the Taliban take away my basic right to education!"

Well done, Malala.

Then the Taliban took over the area and began attacking girls' schools. Malala, aged eleven and supported by her father, gave a speech on the importance of education.

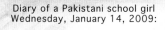

Diary of a Pakistani school girl
Wednesday, January 14, 2009:

--- I MAY NOT GO TO SCHOOL AGAIN ---
I was in a bad mood while going to school because winter vacations are starting from tomorrow. The principal announced the vacations but did not mention the date the school was to reopen. This was the first time this has happened.

The next year, with her parents' approval, Malala started a blog for the BBC about life under the Taliban.

The Taliban are beating people in the streets.

They will not hurt a child.

Even after Malala was revealed as the blogger, she kept speaking out for her right to education.

Don't go home yet. Let's stay and chat. It might be our last day at school.

I'm too scared.

As time went on, the Taliban's control of Swat increased. They destroyed more girls' schools, and fewer of Malala's friends dared to attend school.

Surely, the Taliban will not harm a child—but they might hurt you, Papa.

Malala was becoming well known, and she began to receive death threats. But she was more frightened for her father, an anti-Taliban activist.

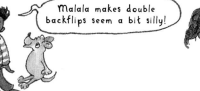

Malala makes double backflips seem a bit silly!

No, you've got to have fun!

Malala's whole family deserves a huge cheer.

"Which one of you is Malala?"

But on October 9, 2012, as fifteen-year-old Malala traveled home from school, a man boarded the bus and shot her in the head. He also injured two of her friends.

Malala was alive but in critical condition. After undergoing surgery in Pakistan, she was flown to Birmingham, England, for further treatment.

"I cannot believe how much love people have shown me."

WELCOME MALALA

Malala received messages of support from around the world, and by March 2013 she was well enough to start school in Birmingham.

"One child, one teacher, one book, and one pen can change the world."

On her sixteenth birthday, Malala gave her first speech to the United Nations, about children's education. Everyone applauded her bravery.

"Hooray for you, Malala Yousafzai!"

"I raise my voice not so that I can shout, but so that those without a voice can be heard."

"Thank you, Malala. You are our champion!"

Malala and her family haven't been able to return to Pakistan, and they miss their beautiful homeland. Despite the Taliban's continued threats, Malala still speaks up for every child's right to quality education, equal rights for women, and peace throughout the world. In October 2014, Malala became the youngest-ever winner of the Nobel Peace Prize. Malala is proof that one voice of passion and truth, however young and seemingly insignificant, can be heard and can make a difference!

"Let's cheer for everyone who speaks for those without a voice!"

"Three cheers and more! Because of you, we can!"

"Woofy!"

Malala's two friends recovered well from their injuries.

Malala's favorite color is purple, and she likes cupcakes and chocolate but not candy!

Malala could not have achieved any of this without her family's support.

Indian children's rights activist Kailash Satyarthi shared the Nobel Peace Prize with Malala.

# HOORAY FOR LEADERS & WORLD CHANGERS!

President of Liberia and Nobel Peace Prize-winner Ellen Johnson Sirleaf (born 1938) was the first female elected head of state in Africa.

Queen Elizabeth II (born 1926) is the only British monarch to have reigned longer than Queen Victoria!

Dorothy Height (1912–2010) was an activist who fought for the rights of African-American women.

An African-American teenager named Claudette Colvin (born 1939) had bravely refused to give up her seat nine months before Rosa Parks, but it was Rosa's action that gave rise to the mass protests.

## HATSHEPSUT
### Egyptian Pharaoh
### (C. 1508–1458 BCE)

Egypt thrived under this noble woman's reign for more than twenty years. She ruled wearing men's clothing, including the pharaoh's false beard!

## ELIZABETH FRY
### English Prison Reformer
### (1780–1845)

Shocked by the filthy and cramped cells for women and children at Newgate Prison, Elizabeth improved conditions and organized schooling for the children and work for their mothers.

*This can't go on!*

## QUEEN VICTORIA
### Queen of the United Kingdom of Great Britain & Ireland & Empress of India
### (1819–1901)

Victoria ruled for sixty-four years! She came to symbolize the Victorian Age and its strict moral values.

## EMMELINE PANKHURST
### British Suffragette
### (1858–1928)

Emmeline helped found the Women's Social and Political Union, whose members fought for the right to vote and were called "suffragettes." American women got the vote in 1920.

## EDITH COWAN
### Australian Politician & Social Campaigner
### (1861–1932)

Edith campaigned for women's and children's rights. In 1921, she became the first woman to be elected to an Australian parliament.

## GOLDA MEIR
### Israeli Politician
### (1898–1978)

Golda was dedicated to helping displaced Jewish people, through both diplomacy and fund-raising. She became the first female prime minister of Israel in 1969.

## SAINT TERESA OF CALCUTTA
### Albanian Nun
### (1910–1997)

"Mother" Teresa dedicated her life to the poor in India. She won the Nobel Peace Prize, and in 2016 she was declared a saint.

*"Spread love everywhere you go."*

**WHITES ONLY!**

*I've had a long day too.*

## ROSA PARKS
### American Civil Rights Activist
### (1913–2005)

In 1955, Rosa broke Alabama state law by refusing to give up her bus seat to a white person. Her arrest sparked protests that resulted in the racial segregation laws of the state being declared unconstitutional.

## BARBARA CASTLE
### British Politician
### (1910–2002)

Barbara introduced the Equal Pay Act in 1970 and fought for social justice at a time when British politics was dominated by men.

**KEEP BLACKBURN BOOMING!**

*"In politics, guts is all!"*

**VOTE LABOR**

*These women are overwhelmingly brilliant!*

*No, most of them are ordinary, but do the extraordinary.*

What about all the amazing women journalists who bring us news stories?

My flock has them covered—just look down below!

## SIRIMAVO BANDARANAIKE
### Sri Lankan Politician
(1916–2000)

Sirimavo was the modern world's first female head of government! She was prime minister of Ceylon and Sri Lanka three times.

"Practice simple living, decorum, and dignity."

"Forgiveness is a virtue of the brave."

## INDIRA GANDHI
### Prime Minister of India
(1917–1984)

Indira was the first elected female prime minister of India. She was in power for fifteen years, and her agricultural policies helped to provide food for many poor people. However, not all her decisions were popular, and she was assassinated in October 1984.

American Nellie Bly (1864–1922) pioneered investigative journalism.

## EDITH WINDSOR
### American Activist for Lesbian, Gay, Bisexual & Transgender Rights
(1929–2017)

Edith fought for equal tax laws for partners in heterosexual and same-sex marriages.

"The way to right wrongs is to turn the light of truth upon them."

## IDA B. WELLS
### American Journalist & Civil Rights Activist
(1862–1931)

Ida was an investigative journalist who exposed injustices against African-Americans. Her reports revealing the violence faced by African-Americans, particularly in the southern United States, led to her newspaper offices being attacked, but it didn't stop her from being a voice against prejudice her entire life.

Irish journalist Orla Guerin (born 1966) has won many honors, including a Most Excellent Order of the British Empire award.

## SHIRIN EBADI
### Iranian Lawyer
(born 1947)

Shirin has fought for democracy and human rights in Iran. She was also the first female judge in Iran and was awarded the Nobel Peace Prize in 2003.

"Nothing useful and lasting can emerge from violence."

## DIANA, PRINCESS OF WALES
### British Charity Campaigner
(1961–1997)

Diana was known as "the People's Princess." She supported over one hundred charities.

She was queen of our hearts!

## SHERYL SANDBERG
### American Executive, Activist & Author
(born 1969)

Sheryl was the first woman to serve on Facebook's board of directors. She is the founder of the Lean In Foundation, which supports women.

"Until women are as ambitious as men, they're not going to achieve as much as men."

Kate Adie (born 1945) and Lindsey Hilsum (born 1958) are English journalists known for broadcasting from war zones.

## MARGARET THATCHER
### British Prime Minister
(1925–2013)

Margaret was the first female British prime minister. She led the country from 1979 to 1990.

"Don't follow the crowd; let the crowd follow you."

## THANDIWE CHAMA
### Zambian Children's Rights Activist
(born 1991)

Thandiwe's school closed when she was eight years old. Determined to have an education, she led her classmates on a walk to find another school! She won the International Children's Peace Prize in 2007.

Sorry, we have no teachers.

CLOSED

Follow me — we'll find another school!

Clare Hollingworth (1911–2017), an English journalist, was one of the first female war correspondents.

What will you do, Dot?

Just be me!

Well, that's extraordinary enough for me!

Woof!

# HOORAY for ATHLETES & CREATIVES!

You want creative? Just take a look at my nest!

I like the American poet Emily Dickinson (1830–1886). Her poetry was published after her death.

I'm chirping for Yuna Kim (born 1990), a South Korean figure skater. She has beaten world-record scores eleven times!

Let's chirp for Chantal Petitclerc (born 1969), Canada's greatest wheelchair racer in the Paralympic Games, with twenty-one medals, including fourteen golds!

Beyoncé (born 1981) is an American singer-songwriter whose hugely popular music often carries a political message.

## CHARLOTTE, EMILY & ANNE BRONTË
### English Writers
(1816–1855, 1818–1848, 1820–1849)

These three sisters wrote classics such as *Jane Eyre*, *Wuthering Heights*, and *The Tenant of Wildfell Hall*. They wrote under pen names to disguise the fact that they were women, since only men were taken seriously as authors at this time.

## HARRIET BEECHER STOWE
### American Writer & Abolitionist
(1811–1896)

Harriet's novel *Uncle Tom's Cabin*, about the terrible life of an enslaved African-American, caught people's attention and raised awareness about the fight to abolish slavery.

"Never give up."

## ENHEDUANNA
### Sumerian Poet
(2285–2250 BCE)

Enheduanna is the world's first known author. She was a high priestess who wrote poetry.

## BEATRIX POTTER
### English Writer, Illustrator & Conservationist
(1866–1943)

Beatrix is best known for her beautifully illustrated animal stories. She taught herself to be a natural scientist, writer, and illustrator.

| THE TALE OF PETER RABBIT | THE TALE OF JEMIMA PUDDLE-DUCK | THE TAILOR OF GLOUCESTER | THE TALE OF THE FLOPSY BUNNIES |

## CHIMAMANDA NGOZI ADICHIE
### Nigerian Writer & Poet
(born 1977)

Chimamanda is an award-winning writer who believes stories can help us understand other people's cultures.

## LOTTIE DOD
### British Tennis, Hockey, Archery & Golf Star
(1871–1960)

Lottie is the youngest woman to have won the Wimbledon Ladies' Singles Championship, at age fifteen. She also played field hockey for England and won an Olympic silver medal in archery.

## FANNY BLANKERS-KOEN
### Dutch Athlete
(1918–2004)

Fanny was voted the greatest female athlete of the twentieth century! She was a sprinter and hurdler, and won four gold medals in the 1948 Olympics.

*zoooooooom!*

## TRISCHA ZORN
### American Swimmer
(born 1964)

"The most important thing was to be recognized and known as a good sportsman."

Blind from birth, Trischa is the most successful athlete ever in the Paralympic Games. She has won forty-one gold, nine silver, and five bronze medals.

KING'S CROSS
## J. K. ROWLING
### English Writer
(born 1965)

J. K. is well known for her Harry Potter books. They are the best-selling series in history!

## ISADORA DUNCAN
### American Dancer
(1877–1927)

Isadora is known as the "Mother of Modern Dance." She broke the rigid rules of ballet and danced in bare feet!

I think I might be a dancer.

Yes, dancing's fun.

Or a jockey. They're always men.

## ANNA PAVLOVA
### Russian Ballet Dancer
#### (1881–1931)

Anna danced with delicacy and grace, amazing audiences around the world.

## MISTY COPELAND
### American Ballet Dancer
#### (born 1982)

Misty is the first African-American female principal dancer with the American Ballet Theatre.

## CLARA SCHUMANN
### German Musician & Composer
#### (1819–1896)

Clara studied music from the age of five. She played the piano and quickly gained a reputation as a child prodigy.

## ARETHA FRANKLIN
### American Singer, Songwriter & Musician
#### (1942–2018)

Aretha started singing at age five. She became known as the "Queen of Soul" for her wonderful voice.

## EVELYN GLENNIE
### Scottish Percussionist
#### (born 1965)

Evelyn is a famous deaf percussionist who hears and feels sound through other parts of her body.

## MIRIAM MAKEBA
### South African Singer & Civil Rights Activist
#### (1932–2008)

Miriam helped make African music popular around the world. She was exiled from South Africa after campaigning against apartheid.

## MARY QUANT
### Welsh Fashion Designer
#### (born 1934)

"I'm not my mother!"

During the 1960s, Mary's fun fashion designs, like the miniskirt and hot pants, gave young people their own style. No more dressing like Mom and Dad!

## ZAHA HADID
### Iraqi-British Architect
#### (1950–2016)

Zaha has a worldwide reputation as one of the geniuses of contemporary architecture. She won many prestigious prizes for her extraordinary and diverse buildings.

## AUDREY HEPBURN
### British Actress & Philanthropist
#### (1929–1993)

"Be happy!"

Audrey is a screen legend and multiple award winner. In the late 1980s, she retired from films to work for UNICEF and was later awarded the Presidential Medal of Freedom.

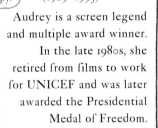

## PAULA REGO
### Portuguese Artist
#### (born 1935)

"I'm drawing . . ."  "my friends!"

Many of Paula's amazing prints and paintings are based on traditional fairy tales told to her by her grandmother. As a child she drew on her bedroom floor!

## AUGUSTA SAVAGE
### American Sculptor & Civil Rights Activist
#### (1892–1962)

Augusta began sculpting clay animals as a child. She eventually won a scholarship to an art school, where she excelled. She helped found the Harlem Artists' Guild to support other African-American artists. Augusta spent her later years teaching and inspiring others.

"Daddy never wanted me to be an artist."

## ELISABETTA SIRANI
### Italian Painter
#### (1638–1665)

At a time when women were expected to be wives and mothers, Elisabetta was a successful painter and engraver by the age of seventeen! She also established an academy for other female artists.

"Oh, no, they're not! There are lots of fantastic women jockeys."

"Well, I don't suppose the horses care what gender you are!"

"Neigh, we don't!"

Bravo Yuan Yuan Tan (born 1977) from China, who started ballet school at eleven and has been delighting audiences ever since.

Chirp for the Indian singer Chithra (born 1963). She has won lots of awards and sung like a bird in twelve languages!

I'm chirping for Bette Davis (1908–1989), a great Hollywood star and the first female president of the Academy of Motion Picture Arts and Sciences!

Nora Ephron (1941–2012) was an award-winning American writer, film producer, and director. She fought for women's rights both in front of and behind the camera. Chirp!

# HOORAY FOR SCIENTISTS, PIONEERS & ADVENTURERS!

Tweeting Marianne North (1830–1890), an English botanical biologist and artist who traveled the world, painting and discovering new plants!

A chirp for Ada Lovelace (1815–1852), an English mathematician known as the first computer programmer — she was way ahead of her time!

Elizabeth Blackwell (1821–1910) was the first woman in America to become a doctor — that is a real chirp!

Chirps for the Dutch sailor Laura Dekker (born 1995), the youngest person to circumnavigate the globe single-handed. She was sixteen, and it took 518 days!

## JANE GOODALL
### English Primatologist & Animal Rights Activist
### (born 1934)

Jane has spent more than fifty years studying wild chimpanzees and has shown how similar to humans they are. She is a passionate supporter of conservation.

## BIRUTÉ GALDIKAS
### Canadian Primatologist & Conservationist
### (born 1946)

Biruté is one of the world's leading experts on orangutans — very clever great apes with startling red hair. She works to preserve their tropical rain-forest habitat.

## CHARLOTTE AUERBACH
### German Zoologist & Geneticist
### (1899–1994)

Charlotte fled to Edinburgh from Nazi Germany. She became one of the first scientists to understand the dangers of nuclear radiation.

## RITA LEVI-MONTALCINI
### Italian Neurobiologist
### (1909–2012)

Rita won the Nobel Prize in Physiology or Medicine for her discovery of how nerve cells grow. Her work led to a better understanding of many medical problems.

## ROSALIND FRANKLIN
### English Scientist
### (1920–1958)

Rosalind's groundbreaking X-ray images helped in the discovery of the structure of DNA. DNA carries genes from one generation to the next.

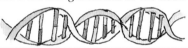

## ELIZABETH GARRETT ANDERSON
### English Physician & Suffragette
### (1836–1917)

Elizabeth enrolled as a nurse at medical school, and after much opposition, she eventually qualified as a doctor. She went on to found a hospital for women and became the first dean of a British medical school, the first female physician in France, the first woman to be elected to an English school board, and the first female mayor and magistrate in England!

"I could not live without some real work."

## RACHEL CARSON
### American Marine Biologist & Conservationist
### (1907–1964)

Rachel's book *Silent Spring* challenged the use of pesticides and encouraged a global environmental movement.

## SELLAPPAN NIRMALA
### Indian Microbiologist
### (born 1953)

As a microbiology student, Sellappan discovered the first cases of HIV, which causes AIDS, in India. Screening and prevention programs that followed saved lives.

## GERTRUDE BELL
### English Explorer, Academic, Spy, Writer & Archaeologist
### (1868–1926)

"It's so nice to be a spoke in the wheel."

Gertrude explored and mapped such places as Mesopotamia and Arabia and helped found the modern Iraqi state. She even had an Alpine peak named after her: Gertrudspitze! At a time when most women never left home, this was all highly unusual, but Gertrude was brave, intelligent, and fearless!

Did you know this is the last page that describes people, Dot?

Yes, Abe. Sad, isn't it?

What shall we do now?

## EDITH CAVELL
### English Nurse
(1865–1915)

As a nurse in German-occupied Belgium during World War I, Edith risked her life by helping French and English soldiers escape. She was arrested and executed.

## JANE HAINING
### Scottish Missionary
(1897–1944)

Jane refused to leave her pupils, many of whom were Jewish, in Hungary during World War II. She stayed with them until she was arrested. She died in Auschwitz.

## VLADKA MEED
### Member of the Jewish Resistance in Poland
(1921–2012)

Vladka was born into a Jewish family. She pretended to be Aryan to help families escape the Nazis and to try to save them from being taken to a concentration camp.

Well, three chirps for them!

## ELIZABETH KENNY
### Australian Nurse
(1880–1952)

Elizabeth trained herself in nursing and traveled into the wilderness to see patients. She pioneered a treatment for the disease polio, which saved many children from permanent paralysis.

## JUNKO TABEI
### Japanese Mountaineer
(1939–2016)

In 1975, Junko became the first woman to reach the summit of Mount Everest. She was also the first woman to climb the highest peak on every continent!

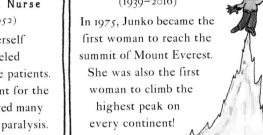

## VALENTINA TERESHKOVA
### Russian Astronaut
(born 1937)

In 1963, Valentina, a former textile worker, became the first woman in space. She was twenty-six years old and orbited Earth forty-eight times in her spaceship *Vostok* 6. She logged more flight time than any astronaut before her.

And a chirp for Amy Johnson (1903–1941), the English pilot who was the first woman to fly alone from Britain to Australia!

## SUSAN LA FLESCHE PICOTTE
### Omaha Physician and Reformer
(1865–1915)

Susan was the first Native American woman to earn a medical degree, and she fought for the Omaha Nation's legal rights.

Humans might chirp for American Marion Donovan (1917–1998), who invented the waterproof disposable diaper. Birds don't bother with those!

"Play is the work of the child."

## MARIA MONTESSORI
### Italian Physician & Educator
(1870–1952)

Maria developed an educational method based on the idea that children learn through play. She opened her first Montessori school in 1907, and there are now thousands worldwide!

## MARGARET KNIGHT
### American Inventor
(1838–1914)

While working in a textile mill at age twelve, Margaret saw a worker injured and came up with her first invention: a safety device for textile looms!

In 1871, she received her first patent, for a machine that made flat-bottomed paper bags. She went on to receive over twenty patents and conceive more than a hundred inventions.

Maybe you could invent something?

Birds can chirp for American Ruth Wakefield (1903–1977), who is credited with having invented the chocolate-chip cookie!

"If it's a good idea, go ahead and do it!"

## GRACE MURRAY HOPPER
### American Computer Scientist
(1906–1992)

Grace was a rear admiral in the U.S. Navy as well as a computer scientist. Her imaginative work in programming computers paved the way for nonmathematicians to use computers.

Call down all those chirping birds and shout:

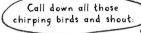

HOORAY FOR WOMEN AND OTHER ASSORTED SENTIENT BEINGS!

## Dear Reader,

Once upon a time, I used to dream of a chocolate bar that would never end. Then, while I was writing about these truly amazing girls and women, I began to dream of a book with enough pages for every single trailblazer. Sadly, the chocolate bar never happened and the book didn't either, so I just had to choose my favorite inspirational women. I do hope you enjoyed reading about them.

These incredible individuals come from all backgrounds and all nations and are all ages. It is impossible to say who are the most important — it really depends on your own beliefs and interests. But I am sure that at least some of the girls and women in this book will fill you with wonder. They have certainly reminded me that, whether you are a boy or a girl, you are never too young or too old to change the world!

With luck and inspiration,
Marcia

QUESTION: How many women do you think I had to leave out?

ANSWER: Thousands. One of my bird friends has a list of some of them. My other bird friend has a blank banner so that you can add all the women and girls who have inspired YOU. I wonder who you will add.

Spice Girls

Vita Sackville-West

# INDEX